For Robert Gleeson, a brother like no other.—B.G.
This is dedicated to the ones I love: Marlene and Molly.—R.M.

Library of Congress Cataloging in Publication Data
Gleeson, Brian.
Paul Bunyan / by Brian Gleeson; illustrated by Rick Meyerowitz.
Summary: Recounts the exploits of the legendary giant logger and his big blue ox Babe.
ISBN 0-88708-142-8: $14.95.—
ISBN 0-88708-143-6 (book and cassette package): $19.95
1. Bunyan, Paul (Legendary character)— Juvenile literature.
[1. Bunyan, Paul (Legendary character) 2. Folklore—United States.
3. Tall tales.] I. Meyerowitz, Rick, 1943- ill. II. Title.
PZ8.1.G4594Pau   1990
398.22'0973—dc20
[E]   90-8558

Written by
Brian Gleeson

Illustrated by
Rick Meyerowitz

PAUL BUNYAN

Rabbit Ears Books

A lot of people will tell you about Paul Bunyan like they know the straight story. But they don't know an ax handle from an ox yoke in my book. Shoot, ninety-nine-point-nine percent of them wasn't even there. Well I was, by Jiminey.

Paul Bunyan ran the crackest loggin' outfit there ever was. Paul flat-out invented loggin', and by the time he got done, the United States was fit for livin'.

Listen up, and I'll tell you about Paul Bunyan, the greatest loggin' man there ever was.

Now, first time I saw Paul Bunyan was the Winter of the Blue Snow. Me and the boys were sittin' in our cabin, huddled around the pot-belly stove. Outside, the snow was fallin' fast, furious, and blue. That's right. It's a fact, the snow came outta the sky as blue as a robin's egg. That's why they called it the Winter of the Blue Snow.

Pancakes was our dinner for the three-hundred-and-tenth night in a row. We was concentrating on talkin' and chewin' with our mouths closed, when it started thunderin' outside.

Then I seen him. He was comin' through the woods, his eye level with the treetops, pushin' pines out of his way like they was cornstalks. And he was carryin' the biggest, mightiest, dang-darndest ax I ever seen. The blade looked to be a hammered-down locomotive—I ain't a-kiddin' ya, and there was no drinkin'!

We all ran outside to get a better look at what was coming our way. And there he stood, large as a mountain.

"Sorry to intrude, boys," he said, real friendly-like. "Name's Paul Bunyan. What do you fellas got cookin'? I've been eatin' beans all winter long, and when I got a whiff of your vittles, I had to stop by."

Well, now, we happened to have the greatest cook this side of Kalamazoo: Hot Biscuit Sally. And her pancakes were such good eatin' that we had 'em mornin', noon, and night. So Sal made up a king-sized batch of pancakes for our guest, and in no time at all he was eatin' and talkin'.

"I'm clearin' the timber off of Sulfur Mountain," Paul explained.

Me and the boys knowed that Sulfur Mountain was so steep that a person trying to walk up it would fall over backwards.

"You mean you're clearin' off Sulfur Mountain by yourself?" I says.

"Yup," says Paul.

The boys didn't know what to think. Either this lad had beans in his head, or he knowed a few things about loggin' that we didn't.

Brimstone Bill was gettin' a little hot under the collar. Brimstone could cuss a blue streak, and he got especially perturbed when he thought a body was braggin'.

"How in tarnation do you expect us to believe that you is clearin' that land by your lonesome?" he snarled.

"I always work alone," said Paul.

"Dad-blame-it!" cried Brimstone. "Then show us how you does it, 'cause I think you're full of soup!"

"The only thing I'm full of right now is pancakes. And I'm feelin' the need for some exercise," said Paul, pattin' his belly and stretchin'. He got up, hefted his ax, and walked into the woods.

"Alrighty, boys, stand clear."

Paul spat into his hands and choked the end of his ax handle. He wound up and swung. He felled twenty-three trees with that first swing. Any one of those trees would have taken you or me at least six hours of choppin'.

Then he got his rhythm, and he started swingin' like a tornado goin' through a toothpick factory. Paul cleared forty acres during his little demonstration, and when the dust settled, any trees that were left standin' took one look around and laid down in fright.

"Well, that's how I do it," says Paul.

He wasn't braggin', either. That boy was just the biggest, bestest, toughest, strongest, ding-dandiest logger there ever was. And that's how we all come to join up with Paul during the Winter of the Blue Snow.

One fine winter's day, while Paul was out scoutin' the countryside, he came across a baby ox, buried in the blue snow. Poor little feller was froze stiff as a plank. Paul dug him out of the drift. That calf had been in the snow so long that his hide was dyed solid blue. Paul blew three warm breaths into the calf, and that critter opened his eyes like he'd just been born.

Well, sir, when he looked up with them big blue eyes, somethin' inside of Paul began to melt. Paul Bunyan was a strappin' man, and stronger than a grizzly bear, and when he cradled that blue ox calf in his arm, he was as gentle as an angel.

"Now there's nothin' to worry about—I'm takin' care of you, babe, and I always will."

That's what everybody called the calf from then on: Babe. From the git-go, Babe ate a ton of grain a day, and was always lookin' for more. The fellers noticed that if they watched Babe for five minutes, they could see him grow right before their eyes. By the time Babe stopped growin', the distance between the tips of his horns measured one-hundred-forty-two ax handles, four bottles of sassafrass soda, a plug of chewin' tobacco, and a hard-boiled egg.

W̲e was cuttin' through the woods like nobody's business, when one day Paul got a letter from Teddy Roosevelt, the President of the United States. Seems Mr. Roosevelt was in a fix, and he needed a hand.

This is how the letter read:

"Well, if that ain't a kick in the britches," Paul said to the boys. "But if that's what the President wants, then that's what he's gonna get."

And with that, Paul dashed off a letter to Teddy Roosevelt:

The Woods
Somewhere
near
Minnesota

Dear Mr. President,

Consider the job DONE.
I'll take care of clearing
The Dakotas, presently,
forthwithly, hence.
Sincerely,
Paul Bunyan
Logger

In those days, the Dakotas were one gigantic forest, so thick with trees you had to pry your way in. There wasn't a lick of open land in the entire territory. The trees were tall and fat, and the wood was so hard you'd dull your ax with just a single swing. Clearin' the Dakotas was the toughest lumber job there ever was, even for Paul Bunyan and his men.

Didn't take long for word to get around that Paul was doing some serious work out there. Loggers started comin' out of the woodwork to work those woods with Paul's crew.

Johnny Inkslinger was the accountant for Paul's loggin' enterprise, and even he couldn't count all the men. The loggers slept in bunk beds with ten decks. So Johnny tried countin' the bunks and multiplyin' by ten to figure the number of men employed. He gave up countin' at ten thousand, six hundred and twenty-three. That's a lot of men.

Boardin' the boys was an even bigger problem. Poor Hot Biscuit Sally was makin' pancakes six ways to Christmas, tryin' to keep everybody fed.

"Paul," she said, "I've burned out three griddles this mornin' alone, and some of our boys still don't have their breakfast. I don't want any logger goin' without pancakes. Now what are we gonna do about it?"

"Sounds like we need a bigger griddle," Paul replied.

So Paul had Ole Jolson, the blacksmith, melt down fifty-three dozen steel plows, and forge a griddle that was an acre-and-a-half across…well, close to that.

Paul and Babe hauled it back to camp. When the two of 'em got back to the peak of Thunder Mountain, Paul decided to ride the griddle the rest of the way.

"Look out below," he yelled. With that, he took off, ridin' the griddle, and givin' out a whoop and holler that darn near made the needles of the pine trees thread themselves, and rattled the teeth in the heads of every man, woman, and beast in the territory. He roared down that mountain, slicin' through the trees and kickin' up boulders, sprayin' them this way and that, and just about scarin' the pants off everything and everybody in his path.

Paul tore into camp, followed by an avalanche of freshly cut trees, hanging on to that griddle for dear life. It was spinnin' like a top, and as it spun, it dug out a hole in the earth under it, fifty-seven feet, four-and-a-quarter inches deep.

The avalanche of twenty-two-thousand logs filled that hole just as the griddle flopped down over it. The heat from the spinning caused the logs to catch fire, and it wasn't long before Hot Biscuit Sal was makin' her first batch of pancakes on her new griddle.

Paul had us build a tank on a tower so Sal could just open a chute and pour the pancake batter right onto the griddle. To grease it, Paul had twenty-six men strap hunks of bacon to their feet and skate on it. I guess you could say we was eatin' a lot of pancakes in Dakota.

With Paul choppin', and Babe totin', the two of them made the perfect loggin' team. Paul would drop a couple of hundred trees onto Babe's sled, and would whisper sweetly into Babe's ear, and Babe would yank that load clear into tomorrow. That ox pulled that sled so hard, he would straighten the chain that held it into a solid iron bar. Ole Jolson had to make a new chain every week, 'cause Babe burned out so many of them.

Havin' an animal that big around camp did present its share of problems. Once, Babe was swattin' bull flies off his back with his tail, when he caught Brimstone Bill between the moustaches, and sent him clear over the ridge. Brimstone got up, cussin' and swearin', aimin' to show Babe who was the boss bullwhacker and who was the ox. When Brimstone got back to camp, Babe just gave him one of his big love licks on the face, and Brimstone melted like butter.

For weeks that fall, the rain poured down in buckets, and we was in mud up to our knees. One night, frightened by lightning, Babe broke out and ran all over the countryside, clear into Minnesota. By morning, his king-sized hoof prints had filled up with rainwater, creatin' a lake out of every single one of 'em. That's why there's ten-thousand lakes in Minnesota to this very day. It was Babe who done it.

President Teddy Roosevelt wanted the Dakotas cleared by spring. Word was out that settlers was already headin' out there, ready to move in. We was loggin' faster than a hog eats supper, but come February, we wasn't even halfway through. There was no way our crew was goin' to complete the job by spring. We were gettin' desperate.

But then a lucky thing happened. Spring never came that year. Folks called it the Year of Two Winters 'cause there was one winter right after the other. On the Fourth of July, it was forty-five degrees below zero, and August was even colder.

On the one hand, havin' two winters gave Paul more time to log off Dakota. On the other hand, bein' doubly cold didn't make it any easier gettin' the job done. It was so cold that Paul's orders to his men froze in mid-air. Even Brimstone Bill's cussin' failed to burn anybody's ears.

It was bleak goin' toward the end of that second winter. Paul still had a third of the Dakotas left to log with only two weeks till spring. Paul and his loggers were slowed to a standstill by the huge pile of cut trees. We were havin' a darn-awful time haulin' the timber out of there, 'cause the road was so crooked. The road not only had S-turns and Z-turns, and U-turns, it had turns shaped like every letter in the dad-blame alphabet, including a few that ain't even been invented yet.

Paul had to do somethin' about that road. So he sat and gave it some thought. And while he thought, he tapped on the ground with his ax. The faster he tapped, the faster he thought, until he was tappin' and thinkin' up a storm. Rocks was rollin' this way and that, and the ground was heavin' up and down in the weirdest shapes you ever saw. Suddenly, Paul leaped up and cried out, "Sufferin' sequoias! I got it!" And this was his idea.

He hooked up Babe to the far end of the road, and gave the blue ox the word to pull. It was that simple. Babe started gruntin', and snortin', and pawin', and pullin', and, wouldn't you know it, the road started to move out. That little bit of give in the road was all Babe needed to feel. He just started marchin' in a straight line, draggin' that road behind him, straightenin' it as true as a crow flies.

As for that strange land Paul created with his tappin', well, we called it the Badlands on account of no one could ever figure out how to live there. Once Babe straightened out the road, Paul Bunyan and his men worked day and night to keep on schedule. There were no breaks for chow, and no sleepin'. Paul chopped so fast that his ax blade grew red-hot, and threw off sparks that lit the night sky like fireworks.

When the rooster crowed at the break of dawn on the first day of spring, Paul felled the last tree in the Dakotas. He had kept his bargain with Teddy Roosevelt.

Paul let loose a
victory holler that blew
down all the scrub pines that
his men hadn't bothered to chop.
He was so full of beans 'cause he'd
finished clearin' the Dakotas, he ran up to
the top of Mount Rushmore.

He carved Teddy Roosevelt's face out of
granite with his ax, and then he added the
faces of three other presidents: Washington,
Jefferson, and Lincoln. It was Paul's
way of personalizing the job
for old Teddy, and, now that
the trees was gone, it gave
folks somethin' to look at.

On the horizon, Paul Bunyan saw a wagon train, bringin' settlers to their new homes where the forest once had been.

Paul surveyed the miles of naked plains all around him. You'd have thought he'd have been happy, finishin' off the biggest loggin' job there ever was, but Paul grew downright sad thinkin' how carried away he got, clearin' the Dakota forest.

"Why these settlers will never hear the wind rustlin' through the leaves," Paul said to no one in particular. "They'll never…they'll never get to sit under the shade of an elm tree on an August afternoon."

Paul and Babe headed north that day. Just picked up and went.

Now, Paul Bunyan ain't dead or nothin', y'understand? Shoot! That boy's like a redwood—he just gets bigger and stronger every year. I know, cause I seen him with my own eyes a winter or two ago.

Paul's done loggin', I'll tell ya that. Paul's plantin' trees now, instead of choppin' them down. He told me there wasn't enough trees, and it was a cryin' shame that all the forests were gettin' logged off. He said he's aimin' to correct the situation.

"I chopped a billion-trillion trees," Paul told me. "Now I'm fixin' to plant a billion-trillion."

And if I know him, that's exactly what he'll do, too.

What's that you say? You want to help? Where can you find Paul Bunyan? Well, that's an easy one. He ain't hard to find.

Go on out there to where the woods is the deepest, and the trees the thickest, where the wind sings through the leaves, and the air is rich with the smell of pine: the heart of the forest. That's where Paul is, that's where he was, and doggonit, that's where he'll always be.